Big Is Beautiful

DAVE PARKER

Big Is Beautiful
Copyright 2008

© 2008 David Parker. All rights reserved.

No part of this book may be reproduced, stored in a retrieval system, or transmitted by any means without the written permission of the author.

Edited by Frank DiGiandomenico

All inquires should be addressed to:
DP Biz Entertainment
65 Windmill Road
Poughkeepsie, NY 12601

ISBN: 978-0-557-02463-6

Table of Content

DEDICATION PAGE II
INTRODUCTION III
YOUR FATNESS 1
BARS OF FAT 3
WHY DO YOU LIKE BIG GIRLS? 7
FAT LOVE 12
WHAT IS SEXY? 16
LOVING THE FAT LIFE 19
FOOD 20
GET UP BIG GIRL 21
DON'T TAKE IT 24
TRUTH 28
HELLO, WORLD! 30
I HATE MYSELF 34
HEY, I'M FAT! 36
ONE ROMANTIC NIGHT 38
LET ME LOVE YOU 43
ASHAMED 46
CLOSET 49
SISTERS 51
REFLECTION 54
DON'T SETTLE FOR LESS 59
NEVER BEEN OUT 78
HE WATCHED ME DIE 81
FAT PRIDE 88
A THREE-LETTER WORD 90
BIG IS BEAUTIFUL 93
FAT PASSION 98
ABOUT THE AUTHOR 104

Dedication Page

This collection of poems is dedicated to my beautiful wife, who is a beautiful full-figured lady, and to all plus size and full-figured women, who are beautiful, sexy, fantastic, attractive and terrific.

Big Is Beautiful is in loving memory of a Beautiful Big Diva.

Selma Louise
1948-2005

A beloved mother, sister, aunt, grandmother, friend and entrepreneur.

*"There are truths in these poems, although some are sad,
If you learn something from them, my soul is glad."*

Introduction

In today's society if you are fat you are treated as a social outcast. It seems like fat and beauty cannot go hand in hand. Society has set a standard that says, if you are fat you are not beautiful; you are not sexy, you are not physically appealing. People of size are discriminated against, scorned, mocked, laughed at, disrespected, unappreciated and humiliated. The world has a phobia about big people and it's time for people to get over it.

There is also a double standard between men and women who are big. Society is much more accepting of men who are fat and gives them full respect. On the other hand, women who are fat are ostracized and are automatically grouped in the ugly and unattractive or the "you have a cute face" category. This is a bias distinction between the face and the plus size body; as to say the face is acceptable but the body is not. Hello! The face is a part of the body. This type of distinction is never made for slim women, even though their bodies are not up to society's standard for sexiness. A lot of the problems and pressures that the full-figured women have to deal with in today's society, King size men don't have to face. Notice how fat men are referred to as "King size," while fat women are referred to as "Plus size." Whatever happened to using the phrase "Queen Size?" Sorry, I forgot, that phrase is already reserved for the stocking sizes of Plus size women.

Who says that a slender and a zero percent body mass index is the standard for sexiness and beauty? A few billion people walk the face of this earth and they all have different colors, shapes and sizes. Slim is no longer the only standard for beauty and sex appeal. Plus size women are just as beautiful, just as sexy, and just as attractive as any other woman.

There are millions of men who adore plus size women, but for some reason they are afraid to express their adoration. Men, it is time for us to overcome our fears and begin to privately and publicly show our love and appreciation for our plus size queens who are an essential part of our lives. It's time for society to stop discriminating, degrading and disrespecting our plus size men and women.

Come and explore a world of poetry that addresses some of the issues that plus size women have to encounter. Get a little taste of some of the daily struggles that plus size women have, and the pain that they have to go through. Experience some of the emotional scars that malicious remarks about their size can leave. Read and be challenged to examine the way we have been mistreating and not appreciating some of the most special people in the world.

Your Fatness

Your fatness:
    Is a beauty to behold.
    Gives you strength untold.
    Is heavenly and divine.
    Makes you one of a kind.
    Is adorable.
    Makes you incomparable.
    Is so soft to the touch.
    Means you've been through so much.
    Helps to make you strong.
    Helps you to persevere long.
    Is a gift from God above.
    Makes you sexy and a joy to love.
    Is to be appreciated.
    Can not be abbreviated.
    Is your energy.
    Use it positively.
    Is your motivation.
    Heightens your imagination.
    Is not a stumbling block.
    Is your life's building rock.
    Is not an embarrassment.
    Is your passion for accomplishment.
    Is not an obstacle in life's course.

Is your overcoming force.
Is not a curse in a big size.
Is a blessing in disguise.

Bars of Fat

I'm trapped inside this fat body,
I feel like I'm a nobody!
I hate being so big and fat;
I want to hide in a cave like a bat.

I don't know why God made me this way.
Please make me slim! So slim I pray!
These bars of fat have imprisoned me
I don't want anyone my body to see.

Why can't I resist fattening food?
I'm always in an eating mood.
I hate, I hate this body of mine!
People say things so cruel and unkind.

These bars of fat are holding me back!
I'm in danger of getting a heart attack.
I'm tired of hearing that I have a pretty face;
And whispers about me at the table during grace.

I can't even walk around the block
These bars of fat have my spirit locked.
I'm watching my life pass me by,
All I can do is sit here and cry.

Lord, just take my life and let me die,
I can't seem to resist those delicious pies.
Each passing day, I put on more pounds;
At the rate I'm going, I won't be around!

These bars of fat have imprisoned me.
I hate my life! I hate what I see!
I only I could end it all,
No one will miss me, they don't even call.

My life is a mess! How did I get to this point?
The pain still exists! Why am I smoking this
    joint?
If I don't love me, then why should others care?
My weight has filled my heart with great fear.

Why am I wallowing in self pity?
Why am I sitting here being unwise and acting
    silly?
Why am I allowing my self-esteem to hit the
    floor?
Why can't my pride like the eagle soar?

Maybe it's time for me to get up and act,
And stop feeling sorry because my body's not
    intact.

Its time for me to step up to the plate,
And be the wonderful creature that God did
 create.

These bars of fat are not going to hinder me,
From living my life happy and free!
I'm going to take control of my life!
I know I'll have to struggle with strife.

But I'm determined to make it through!
And stop feeling sorry for myself while singing
 the blues.
I'm going to take it one day at a time,
Lose one by one, these pounds that are mine.

I'll eat less-fattening foods when I dine,
No more greasy meats, especially the fried kind.
I'll get more exercise and move around;
Walk a mile every day, stepping to musical
 sounds.

Every mile that I walk my pounds will reduce
I'll pay attention to the amount of sugar that is in
 my juice.
I won't be extremely obsessive watching
 everything I eat

I'll cut back on the starch and wean myself off of
    candies so sweet.

It's going to be tough to break these bars,
I have the power inside of me to reach the stars.
These bars of fat are obstacles that will be
    removed!
I am determined myself to improve!

These bars of fat will no longer imprison me!
I love myself and I will be free!
I love myself! I'm fat, luscious and lovely!
I love myself! I was made wondrously!

Why Do You Like Big Girls?

I get these questions all the time,
Why do you like the fat kind?
Why do you stray from the norm?
Why are you attracted to the fat form?

Why don't you prefer women who are slender and slim?
Why don't you like girls that resemble Little Kim?
Why do you like girls that are so big?
What is it about them that you dig?

I don't know what people expect me to say;
My heavenly Father created me this way.
People never ask, "Why don't you like thin girls?"
Who made slim the standard for the whole world?

God created slim and big women all precious in His sight.
If you love a big girl; it's not wrong, it's alright!
Variety is the spice of life, so pick who you like.
If your preference is for big girls, that's dynamite!

All the girls that God created are beautiful.

God hates lying lips, so I must be truthful.
When God created big girls He had me in mind.
Big girls are sexy, sassy, feisty and kind.

God gave me the desire for the voluptuous size.
I can't argue with God, because He is all wise.
Big girls are so special, appealing and unique.
They take my breath away, I can hardly speak.

They have personalities that are humble and
   sweet.
They are the nicest people you'll ever meet.
I love the big body and I'm not the only male.
They take my breath away, I can't wait to exhale.

Of all God's women, big girls are my preference.
You want to know why? Take some notes for
   your reference.
I love big girls and I'm not ashamed or shy.
Big girls are the sexiest; I'm going to tell you
   why.

Big bodies have an alluring, captivating elegance;
Lots of comfort and tenderness that adds to the
   romance.
A voluptuous figure is so juicy to hold.

Oh, the joyous warmth when the weather gets
   cold.

A rotund body is so soft and smooth;
One sight, one touch gets me in the mood.
A pudgy stomach is so supple and sleek;
Sparks fly when my lips and her plump lips meet.

One kiss from her luscious lips brings me to my
   knees.
Her generously proportioned body I love to
   squeeze.
That corpulent outline is oh so divine!
It renews my soul, my body and mind.

A chubby chest is an angelic caress.
If you have a big girl you are truly blessed.
I love big girls even though they are overweight.
It adds to our pleasure when we get intimate.

Their look, their feel has such sex appeal.
My desire for big girls cannot be concealed.
So soft, so silky, so tender to the touch;
I love to fondle and cuddle her much.

I cherish the moments when we embrace.
No other woman can take a big girl's place.

But most important of all I tend to find,
Big girls are so amorous, generous and kind.

They're not as fussy as other girls are;
They shine like the stars, but keep trouble afar.
They are so forgiving and bashful at times,
They'll stand by you through good and bad times.

They'll take care of you when you are sick,
Make the most delicious soups, the pot you'll
    want to lick!
They won't sell you out for a nickel or a dime.
I'm so happy to have a big girl that's truly mine!

They are friendly and so much fun to be around.
They can make you smile when you're feeling
    down.
They know where to find the best food and drinks,
So don't prejudge big girls, before you speak,
    think!

Fat girls are attractive and fantastic,
There are so many things about them that are
    terrific.
Their character is gentle, affectionate and unique.
I just love their enchanting bounteous physique!

So now you know why big girls rock!
Close your mouth and don't look shocked!
Now you know why big girls are so irresistible,
Now you know why big girls are so incredible.

Now you know why I love girls with weight,
I hope this sets the record straight!

Fat Love

It takes a special kind of love to love a big girl,
The kind of love that would change the whole
    world.
A love that transcends both shape and size,
It does not pretend or make up lies.

This love is gentle, loving, patient and kind,
It does not change with the passing of time.
It does not speak evil words about your pounds,
Even when no one else is around.

This special kind of love was sent from above,
Because God knew big girls would need special
    love.
God created us all from the same thing,
So Special love spread your wings.

God created us from the dust of the earth,
And every one of us has much worth.
Big girls have an angelic voice,
You need that special love to make them your
    choice.

Fat love will accept you and re-emphasize,

That you are beautiful and special, no matter your size.
Fat love will love you at all cost,
Fat love won't treat you like a puppy that's lost.

Fat love is a love that is not so rare,
It is just a denied love that society fears.
Love yourself and wait to find,
The Fat Lover who is worth your time.

But keep in mind as you wait,
That you will encounter a lot of hate.
People will not appreciate who you are,
They are too blind to perceive that you are a super star.

One word of caution,
That I must mention.
You don't need a man to make you complete.
You are self-sufficient and adorably sweet.

Accept yourself and don't be blue,
You are a wonderful person and that is true.
Let your love shine and glow from within;
Being big is not a sin!

Let your love radiate from without;

Show the world that big is beautiful and there's no doubt!
And when that special love comes along,
He'll stand by your side and help to keep you strong.

You won't have to worry where he is at night,
He'll be lying beside you, holding you tight.
His actions will demonstrate how much he loves,
His speech will be peaceful and harmless like doves.

This special love will come your way,
Just love yourself, trust God for that day.
Love yourself first and you will see,
Your love for you will set you free.

Remember the beauty inside of you,
And just keep on loving and to yourself be true.
And some day you will find,
A man who is worth all of your time.

A man who was given that heavenly touch.
One that adores big girls oh, so much!
A man who will not of you be ashamed,
To hold your hand and to the world proclaim.

That big girls are fantastic, attractive and terrific!
And demonstrate this Fat Love that is so majestic!

What Is Sexy?

What is sexy?
Fat is oh, too sexy!
It is a hundred times better than ecstasy.
It is not only your size that pleases;
Oh, your curves how they appeases.
Yes, big girls are mighty nice!
They can cook a delicious pot of rice.

Yes, I love your body size!
It makes the passion inside of me rise.
Oh, how my hands love to caress,
Your big and voluptuous breasts.
I love to lean against your full-size belly,
It is smooth and firm like jelly.
Your legs so thick and oh so plum!
Makes my muscles go "rupa, tom-tom!"

Oh, I love the way your body glides!
I must have you as my bride.
The softness of your gentle touch,
Makes me want you, oh so much!
The warmth of your embrace,
Makes my heart beat like I just ran a race.

I love to lean upon your chest,
And let my hands roam and caress.
In your softness and tenderness I find,
Relaxing vibes that sooth my mind.
I love your mind, your body and soul.
You make me feel complete and whole.
And when you rub your hand on mine,
It sends tingling sensations down my spine.
I don't need wine to get me into the mood,
Your fatness has already gotten me in the groove.
I love to feel your weight on me,
And make passionate love from six to three.

That's nine hours if you can count,
Big girls require love in large amounts.
Passionate love is what you need;
The stamina of a stallion steed.
Romance with affection and dinner with wine;
With big girls you've got to take your time.

Don't let the lust make you rush,
This is not a simple childhood crush.
You have to take it slow; there is a lot to do.
Plenty of places to kiss and touch too!
Don't worry, you won't have to do all the work,
She'll set you on fire, like you just tasted jerk.

The intense and passionate love that I feel,
Has me begging for your fat appeal.
Your body and passion rocks my world,
Sparks fly as our bodies entangle in an embracing twirl
You make my muscle firm and my toes curl.
That's why, what is sexy is a big girl!

Don't believe all the rumors that you hear,
Making love to you, big girl, will make you swear.
Fat is sexy and does entice!
It adds to sex vigor, gusto and spice.
Fat is sexy! Don't you forget it!
Fat is sexy! Come on admit it!

Loving the Fat Life

I'm so happy with my life,
Because I'm married to a fantastic wife.
I'm living a terrific fat life,
Because of my beautiful big wife.
We have very few disagreements and little strife.
I love being married to a fantastic, plump wife!

Before we part I have to kiss her twice.
When she cooks, she adds the right amount of
    spice.
She seasons the meat, down right nice!
She puts her foot in that peas and rice!
The bread she bakes melts the butter on every
    slice,
And thirst quenching lemonade chilled with ice.

My nights are never lonely or cold.
I feel the warmth when we hold.
She's more precious to me than silver and gold.
The love we share can never be sold.
Our love grows stronger each day we get old.
The fatness of our love is represented by her rolls.

She is caring, loving, gentle and kind.

With a heart so meek, it blows my mind.
We share a love that has an incredible bind.
When I forget, she is always there to remind.
She's that special life partner that's so hard to
 find.
Anywhere I go she is never left behind.

Our love is immeasurable, like the grains of sand.
We live in harmony like a melodious band.
If I knew the fat life would be this grand,
I would not have taken so long to make a stand.
It seems like I'm living in a fairy tale land.
I'm so happy she gave me her hand.

Food

I love to eat and I don't know why.
I love to eat and I'm not shy.
Eating food is one of the finer pleasures in life.
Some people eat because they have a lot of strife,
But I eat because I love to taste good food.
The smell of ham hocks puts me in a happy mood.
God gave us five senses and taste is one,
If I could not taste, life would be no fun.

Get Up Big Girl

Get up big girl from your bed!
Dry your eyes and raise your head!
Just because you're big there's no reason to play
    dead.
You must face this troubled world instead.

I know that people can be really mean.
And laugh about the big people they've seen.
The words they speak cut deep down to your very
    soul.
But big girl you've got to be bold!

Don't let this world stop you from living your
    life!
Because you don't fit the profile of the ideal wife.
There is nothing wrong because you have a lot of
    weight.
People need to stop hating and start to appreciate!

Yes, you've eaten more than your fair share,
And it's hard to find clothes that you can wear.
But that's no reason to stay in bed,
And cry all day and make your eyes red.

Yes, people will mock and call you names;
And laugh at you like it's a game.
Be proud of yourself for who you are!
When you encounter negative people, keep them afar.

You're the only one who can make yourself content.
You have to strive for your betterment!
Don't let your size keep you back,
Restore the confidence that you lack!

So don't hang your head down and frown,
And constantly stare angrily at the ground.
You can accomplish anything you desire to do,
You can fulfill your dreams and here is how to.

Big girls are special; why can't you see?
You have to love yourself before you can be set free!
Believe in yourself and overcome your fears
Encourage yourself even though no one else cheers.

Change the things you don't like, if you can.
Accept what you can't change like a man.
Remove from your mind all negativity,

Retrain your mind to think positively.

Get up big girl, the world is yours to possess,
You only have to strive and give it your best.
Get up big girl and start building your paradise!
Life as a big girl is beautiful and mighty nice!

Don't Take It

Pretty big girls please pay attention.
I have a few thoughts that I think I should
 mention.
Why do you let your man treat you so bad?
Yell and beat you like he's your dad.

Just because you're big and thick,
Is not a reason to be hit with a stick?
Don't let a man push you around,
Or scratch your face and beat you down.

Remember that you are big and round,
So use your weight and squish him down!
Stop letting him treat you like a pig!
Hey, you are lovely even though you are big.

Believe in yourself and you will find,
You are priceless, precious, and one of a kind.
Don't be afraid to pack your bags,
And leave that man with his tail to wag.

Don't put out until you are man and wife.
Shacking up will lead to misery and strife.
Even if you get that diamond ring,

If he really loves you he'll control his thing.

You don't have to argue, fuss and fight;
If he doesn't treat you right just leave that night.
Don't be afraid to be alone,
When you leave, don't ever call his phone!

Big girl, leave that man in jail!
Why don't you stop posting his bail?
You don't need a man to bring you down,
Who treats you badly and smacks you around.

Just because you are big it does not mean,
A man can treat you as he deems.
You deserve to be treated much better than that,
Even though you are heavy and fat.

No matter what size you are,
You should never be shoved into a car.
Why do you put up with that abuse?
Get out of that relationship, there is no excuse!

Time for you to leave, so get your bags packed!
Don't you fear and don't you dare look back!
Pack up your things and leave that man.
Don't tell him a thing; just go as far as you can.

You don't need a man to define you,
And make your face black and blue.
Love doesn't mistreat or abuse,
Or say derogatory things for it's amuse.

Don't let that man back into your life!
He's just going to cause you heartache and strife!
What you need to do is work on you!
Appreciate yourself with love anew!

Discover the beauty that's inside,
And don't let a man push you aside.
You should be treated with love and respect.
Just because you're fat doesn't make you a reject.

Gather strength to persevere from God above.
Spread your wings and fly like a dove.
Appreciate yourself for who you are!
Raise your standards and raise them far!

Don't blame yourself in any way,
From any kind of abuse, just stay away.
If you are in any situation where you're being hit,
Find the determination and courage to just split.

Love and abuse are *not* tightly knit!

Don't you to abuse submit!
There is no justification for abuse that is legit!
Big beautiful girl, please don't take it!

Truth

I am a man who truly finds big girls irresistible.
I cherish big girls, they are so lovable.
Believe in what I'm saying to you,
Trust in my words, they are all true.

I really love big girls a lot!
They can get my fire burning hot!
They know their way around the kitchen.
And cook a mean piece of fried chicken.

They have the key to unlock my heart.
My love for big girls will never part.
Big girls always give more than all the rest.
It's hard to compete in a world where thin seems
    best.

Big girls are always looked down upon,
And people make fun of them in songs.
I don't know why the world is such a mess.
Big girls are always put to the test.

The teasing, the abuse, the jokes prolong,
Society you know that's so wrong!
Discrimination against big girls is very real,

And even their families do fail.

Be bold, be strong and don't give in!
Just be yourself and you will win!
There's amazing beauty in your plus size,
Those who don't know this are not too wise.

Hello, World!

Hello, world! What about me?
Hello, world! Can't you see? I have a big body!
Hello, world! Are you ignoring us?
Big girls are going to have to kick up a fuss.

All of these chairs are way too small.
Especially chairs at the shopping malls.
I know we are not the model type!
I know we are not fluffy and light!

I know we're heavy and most chairs will break.
How many engineers will it take?
To design more things that will accommodate,
And bear the pounds of all my weight.

What's the point of mining steel?
If helping others was not a part of the deal.
Why do you make clothes so small?
There is no reason for us to go to the mall.

This world has people with many different shapes
    and sizes.
It's about time designers begin to realize.
Do I need to shout this from a microphone?

HEY! WHAT ABOUT ME, THE FAT AND BIG BONED?

Society caters to everyone but the plump;
The petite, the tall, the slim, the blind and the dumb.
That is fantastic and to be applauded, I must emphasize.
But what about the people who are big and plus size.

The people who are big you deliberately ignore.
Society does not think big people should sit by the seashore.
We are looked down upon, like freaks or clowns.
They say we are cute, but have extra pounds.

All that does is to insult us more,
And bring our self-esteem crashing down to the floor.
It's really a shame we big girls get treated this way.
Wrong is wrong and discrimination won't pay!

Hello, world! Big girls do exist!
Even though we are not on the top of your list.

Make way for us big girls and you will find,
That we are precious gems that sparkle and shine.

Hello, world, big girls do exists!
We've been treated horribly and now we're
    pissed!
Hello, world! Big girls do exist!
We will not be ignored, we must insist!

Our story of pain has not yet been told,
We have been scorned, put down, and left in the
    cold.
Big is beautiful! What do we lack?
Start making room because Big is back!

Because you are slender and can fit a size 3,
Doesn't mean you are better than me.
We are going to open our mouths and sing,
A pound or two doesn't mean a thing!

Hello, world! We are sick of all the fat jokes,
We are tired of all the demeaning stares from
    folks.
We are fed up with all the insulting comments.
We won't put up with this sub-human treatment!

We are going to hold our heads up high,

Our value, our talent, and our beauty, you will not
 deny!
Hello, world! Being skinny has been the norm.
Hello, world! It's time for education and reform.

Hello, world! You teach that thin is best,
And deny the exquisite beauty big girls possess.
Hello, world! You have been misinformed,
Beauty and sexiness also comes in the big form,

Hello, world! We will no longer subjugate,
Because we have some extra weight.
Hello, world! Being skinny has been the norm.
Unite big girls, we are taking this world by storm!

I Hate Myself

I hate myself because I'm fat!
I don't fit into society's act.
I'm the hidden blob behind the pole.
While the slim girls take the leading roles.
I just don't fit into society's plans,
And no one wants to play with me in the sand.

I cannot eat my meals in peace,
Without someone saying, "That should be your
    last piece!"
I know sometimes I eat too much.
But degrading me doesn't help as such.
Even my so-called friends and family,
Make fun and joke about my big tummy.

Sometimes I try to take insults in stride,
But deep down inside the pain I hide.
I know I'm big, an oversize 14,
But do you really have to be so mean!
I hate that I'm fat and such a large size,
I can never compete for a modeling prize.

It's so hard to find clothes that fit
Comfortably around my big arms and hips.

I have to wear my clothes so tight,
And hold my breath with all my might.
I try to avoid sitting in certain chairs,
Because they may require a few repairs.

I hate myself because I'm fat!
I get treated like a door mat.
People look at me like a big freak.
They giggle, laugh, point and peek.
Sometimes I wonder if they realize,
That they are contributing to my demise.

I took out a knife, to take my life,
Being fat comes with too much strife.
As I put the blade to my neck,
My love for life, those suicidal thoughts wreck.
Don't take your life, you still won't win!
You won't be happy even if you are thin!

You have to accept and love the size that you are!
Embrace the fat, you are still a star!
Love yourself and yourself appreciate,
You are a lovely person even with the weight.
So let the mean words bounce off your chest.
You are big and beautiful and you're the best!

Hey, I'm Fat!

Hey, I'm fat! I'm not going to disappear.
Hey, I'm fat! Say a mean word in my face, if you dare!
Hey, I'm fat! I'm not going to run away.
Hey, I'm fat! I'm here to stay!
Hey, I'm fat! Everyone can see!
Hey, I'm fat! Stop making jokes about me.
Hey, I'm fat! And I can sing.
Hey, I'm fat! I am a sexy thing.
Hey, I'm fat! And I'm overweight!
Hey, I'm fat! I'm happy and so elate!
Hey, I'm fat! Don't put me down.
Hey, I'm fat! Especially when your friends are around.
Hey, I'm fat! I'm a beautiful girl.
Hey, I'm fat! I'm going to tell the world.
Hey, I'm fat! I'm a beautiful person.
Hey, I'm fat! I'm cute, please do mention.
Hey, I'm fat! You better start to appreciate!
Hey, I'm fat! Spread more love and less hate!
Hey, I'm fat! You can't keep me down.
Hey, I'm fat! You've got to love every pound.
Hey, I'm fat! Don't laugh at my rolls.

Hey, I'm fat! I'm a wonderful person, let the truth be told.
Hey, I'm fat! I'm big and gorgeous.
Hey, I'm fat! My body is voluptuous.
Hey, I'm fat! Just give me a chance.
Hey, I'm fat! I can boogie and dance.
Hey, I'm fat! I'm thoughtful and wise.
Hey, I'm fat! Can I get that in King size?
Hey, I'm fat! I want you to know!
Hey, I'm fat! And sometimes I move a bit slow.
Hey, I'm fat! I may not be in the best shape.
Hey, I'm fat! Give me a chance, please stop the hate!
Hey, I'm fat! Don't prejudge me because of my size.
Hey, I'm fat! Give me a chance and you'll realize.
Hey, I'm fat! All the rumors you hear aren't true.
Hey, I'm fat! I'm just like you!
Hey, I'm fat! It's not over till the fat lady sing.
Hey, I'm fat! I just want to say one last thing.
Hey, I'm fat! And you may be thin.
Hey, I'm fat! But you are ugly within.
Hey, I'm fat! I'm one of a kind.
Hey, I'm fat! You need to elevate your mind.
Hey, I'm fat! I don't disrespect you!
Hey, I'm fat! I demand respect too!

One Romantic Night

I can still remember the first night we met,
As I pulled up you were sitting on the steps.
The sky was sprinkled with a million stars,
But your presence shined through by far!

The moon emanated a romantic light,
I was nervous, but full of delight.
The darkness seemed to cover your face,
You waited patiently for me with grace.

As the moonlight exposed the silhouette of your face,
My heart was pounding and accelerated its pace.
As the moonlight disclosed your skin,
That's where my love for you did begin.

Creamy and tender was your skin that shined,
I desired for you to be mine.
Gazing from a distance as you were stepping down,
I noticed you had a lot of pounds.

When I saw your size I hesitated,
You were bigger than I anticipated.

But in an instant that thought was gone,
As the moonlight revealed your radiance, our love
    was born.

It does not matter what size you are,
Your beauty was most spectacular.
The closer you got the moon light revealed,
You were the most attractive big girl, with sex
    appeal.

Love at first sight, oh could it be?
My heart was filled with such glee.
Time stood still as you walked down that path.
With every step you took, you captured my heart.

As you approached, the more I could see,
The bigness of your body was alluring to me.
Your face so beautiful and adorably round,
I almost forgot I was standing on the ground.

As we greeted you stretched out your hand,
I instantly became your number one fan.
And when you placed your hands in mine,
I knew from that moment you would be mine.

You did excite me with much delight,

As the moon set the tone for a romantic night, oh
   so right!
Breathtaking you were, right from the start.
Oh, the passion you ignited deep down in my
   heart.

With silky skin so smooth and tender;
My heart and body I was ready to surrender.
Emotions ran high, excitement so intense!
You aroused all five of my body senses.

You have a stunning body and voluptuous chest,
My eyes could not help but notice; was this a test?
You emanated more splendor than the stars in the
   sky.
I knew I had to have you or I would die!

Your whole essence was full of prettiness,
You were everything I desired and nothing less!
I wanted to continue to hold your hand,
But I had to be the perfect gentleman.

A magical enchantment had surrounded us;
It was composed of romance, love and a sexual
   lust.
I wanted to touch your chubby cheek,
My arousal was over its maximum peek.

Now that we were finally face to face,
I had visions of you dressed in white satin lace.
I looked into your brown eyes and there to find,
That you were exceptional, affectionate, and one
 of a kind.

Your lips so soft I wanted to kiss.
Not kissing you was hard to resist.
Your smile shined with such brilliance and grace,
My X-rated thoughts were impossible to erase.

Your sexy body was not so thin,
And that was a wonderful thing!
Your plus size body has set you apart,
You have already won my heart!

You are what my body craves and my heart's
 desire.
Why is my shirt wet? I can't help but perspire.
Being in your presence is a pleasure and delight,
The moon has released its romance into the night.

Your passion I wanted to consume,
Intensified by the scent of your sweet smelling
 perfume.
You are so weighty, luscious and one of a kind,

Your fatness has intoxicated me, like fine vintage
   wine.

Gaze into my eyes and say you'll be mine;
I promise you that I'll treat you so kind.
I'll love you, honor you and even obey
Till death do us part or whatever comes our way.

Through every pound you may lose or gain,
My love for you shall remain.
Not only in thought, but in deed,
I'll be everything you need.

You are my greatest fantasy
Your love is more addicting than ecstasy.
You are my true love, and it will give me pride.
I love you big girl, would you be my bride?

Let Me Love You

Why are you pretending that nothing's wrong?
I know that big girls are very strong.
But at times we all need a shoulder to cry on,
Please give me a chance to be the one.

I want to hold you when you are feeling down,
Make you smile; I'll be your love clown.
I want to hold you all night
And let you know that everything is going to be alright.

I want to give you a gentle secure embrace,
That will all your hurt and pain erase.
I know you've been disappointed in the past,
Give me a chance and your doubts won't last.

On my chest you can sweetly rest,
And I'll reassure you that big is the best.
I know sometimes you want to be alone,
I'll be your rock, your cornerstone.

I know the pain your weight can bring,
My love will help to ease the sting.
The sensual ness of your weight

I've learned to honor and appreciate.

Your weight has affected your quality of life
Let me help you with your problems and strife.
I know the many tears you've spent
Be brave; I love your inner strength!

Depression and shyness is not the cure
My love for you is pure.
I see the pain that you've been through;
Let me love you, I'm someone new.

Big girl don't cry, the sky will turn back to blue
My love for you is sincerely true.
I know that fat girls have been maimed,
Of your fatness I won't be ashamed.

Your fatness makes me desire you more,
You are the big girl I adore.
Your voluptuous body I want to explore,
Let me love you mi amore.

Look into my eyes and see how I feel inside
I love you no matter how wide.
Just give me a chance to be the man
I will proudly by your side stand.

Let's begin by being friends,
And help your broken heart to mend.
As big as you are,
You are still my bright star.

Even though you are not super-thin,
Give me a chance your heart to win.
I know the big life has a lot of strife
Let me be the superman in your life.

Ashamed

Why am I ashamed to be seen?
In public with the girl of my dreams.
She's so lovely and means the world to me,
But I'm ashamed for people to see.

She stuck with me through the rain and the storm.
She cooks and cleans and keeps me warm.
Even sometimes when I treat her mean,
Her love for me is still bright like a sunbeam.

I don't understand why I feel this way,
I'm just afraid of what people will say.
I have not introduced her to my family,
They will laugh and call me crazy.

Why am I ashamed of my fat girl?
Who stands by me and never swirls.
I know she's fat, but she always has my back.
She makes sure there is nothing that I lack.

She takes good care of me and never frets,
Even though flowers I never get.
When she wants me to go with her to the mall,
I find all kind of excuses and I stall.

We've never gone out to restaurants to eat
I don't want her and my friends to ever meet.
I know that I've been so very wrong
I'm ashamed of my girl friend; I've been with so long.

My love for her won't let me sleep at night,
I've got to treat my big girl right.
Big babe, I'm sorry for all the wrong that I've done.
I apologize for being ashamed of you for so long.

I'm sorry for hurting you in so many ways,
This is going to be the start of a brand new day.
Big babe please put on your dancing shoes,
We are going to the mall for a sexy dress to choose.

We'll walk with your hand in mine
So the world can see that you are mine.
You are fantastic, attractive, and terrific!
Tonight I'm going be so amazingly romantic.

You'll show off your fabulous shape,
So, big babe, please don't be late!
Big baby we are going out tonight!

We are going to wine and dine in the moonlight.

A delicious candlelit dinner for two,
Just me and my big baby, you!
After that we'll go back to our place,
You'll model your gifts of red sexy lace.

The fireplace will be burning bright,
And we'll be up until the morning light.
Girl, I'm sorry that I've been ashamed,
I've been such a jerk and so lame.

You've been so wonderful and remarkable!
Big girl, you are downright just so lovable.
Tonight we are going to make some exhilarating
    magic.
Do I need to get more specific?

Closet

A long time ago before I was 10,
My teacher locked me in a closet and gave me a
    pen.
The closet was dark and creepy inside,
Every day from 8 to 3 o'clock I cried.

I had nightmares both day and night,
From being locked in a closet with no light.
I wonder why I was treated so mean,
I was no different from the other kids I've seen.

I could not figure what was going on,
My life was threatened if I told anyone.
I was a normal kid about 7 or 8,
I did my home work and was never late.

I did not know why my teacher hated me so,
But I decided in the closet I would not go!
One day my teacher opened the closet to put me
    in,
But I refused and was determined that I would
    win!

My teacher got angry and raised her hand,

She was about to slap me and turn my teeth into
   sand.
"Why do you hate me?" I cried, I've done nothing
   wrong.
I've done all my work and I study all night long.

She came to her senses and turned red and blue,
The tears flowed from her eyes and then I knew.
She sat at her desk and gasped for air,
My eyes were opened to a world that's not fair.

You remind me of me when I was young,
You remind me of the hateful teasing songs.
I can't stand to look upon your face,
It's too painful my thoughts to erase.

It was at that moment I realized,
She hated me because of my size.
I ran over to her and gave her a hug,
We cried so much, our tears could fill a jug.

I told her God loves us in spite of our shape and
   size,
Big is beautiful you must realize; big is beautiful
   just to re-emphasize.

Sisters

Sister dear sister, how I love you so!
Sister dear sister, you've caused me a lot of woe!
Sister dear sister, how could you treat me this way?
Sister dear sister, you hurt me with the things that you say.

Sister dear sister, I know that you are smaller than me.
Sister dear sister, I know everyone thinks a model you can be.
Sister dear sister, I know that I'm fat.
Sister dear sister, is that a reason for your lack of tact?

Sister dear sister, you are supposed to be my friend
Sister dear sister, will the fat jokes every end?
Sister dear sister, I thought you understood,
Sister dear sister, I never thought that you could.

Sister dear sister, now I can clearly see,
Sister dear sister, you really don't love me.
Sister dear sister, now I know where I stand,

Sister dear sister, from now on I'll make my own plans.

Sister dear sister, you think that you have broken me,
Sister dear sister, you think that I'm going to flee.
Sister dear sister, insulting me won't help me lose weight.
Sister dear sister, you prefer your friends who fat hate.

Sister dear sister, I know that I'm fat!
Sister dear sister, your insults I will squash flat!
Sister dear sister, I won't let you put me down.
Sister dear sister, you won't replace my smile with a frown!

Sister dear sister, I love me for the way that I am.
Sister dear sister, I'm not going to hide myself like a clam.
Sister dear sister, I'm big beautiful and proud!
Sister dear sister, I don't have to be accepted by the crowd.

Sister dear sister, if you don't like what you see,
Sister dear sister, if my sister you don't want to be

Sister dear sister, just stay away and shut your mouth.
Sister dear sister, don't upset me, you know, or I'll knock you out!

Reflection

As I lie here in bed with my arm around your
  back.
You're so soft to touch and firm to love smack.
I wonder what my life would be like,
If you weren't here to hold me tight.

You are my life's companion who makes me
  happy.
I love you and adore your fat body.
Our family and friends said you would bring me
  strife.
They said you'd be an embarrassment as my wife.

They constantly poured the pressure on,
And treated me with so much scorn.
I was so hurt and confused, that I wanted to die.
I could not sleep at night; all I could do was cry.

The love that I have for you in my heart
Would not allow me from you to depart.
I could not let my fat love go,
I had to let the whole world know.

The feelings I have are not driven by pity,

I truly think that your fatness is pretty.
You know what your fatness does to me,
You know your body I love to see.

You know sympathy can't arouse such attraction.
You know how long my soldier stands at
   attention.
You know what we do when we go to bed at
   night,
You know how we awake basking in the morning
   light.

You've experienced my sexual tension.
Oh the details I won't dear mention.
As I lie next to you, I hear your peaceful snore,
Your big beautiful body I observe and adore.

I always say a prayer when I watch you rest,
That God will bless the big girl I love best.
You have given me so much joy and delight,
You consume my mind when you are out of my
   sight.

You've given me the most precious gift that gives
   great joy,
You gave me precious life, our baby boy.

Four years have gone by, how quickly time does
   fly!
Since we've promised to love each other until we
   die.

Four years is not a major milestone,
But my love for you has surely grown.
I can't imagine you not being in my life.
I can't imagine you not being my wife.

Sleep on, big baby, and get your rest,
Our love will conquer any test.
Before I snuggle up to you and go to sleep
I have to ask the Lord to protect and keep.

Good night, my love, I can't wait for you to wake,
For lunch tomorrow, I think we'll have a picnic
   by the lake.
Have wonderful dreams as you drift in dream
   land.
Big girl, you've made me a very happy man.

Take Advantage

People always try to take advantage of me,
Because they can't get pass the fat that they see.
Some guys think that I'm an easy chic.
Some guys think they can beat me with a stick.

Some guys think they can lead me on,
Get my money and then they are gone.
Some girls think I can't get a man,
They think that I never have any plans.

Some girls think they can steal my man,
Just with the clapping of their hand.
Some girls only want me to hang out,
So their slimness can stand out.

My family always wants me to baby-sit,
They always pop up with their kids, then split.
Friends only call when they have no plans
Guys think they can use me as a one-night stand.

How can I have a life when they are always
    invading mine?
I'm tired of people taking advantage of me all the
    time.

I may not have a man, but I have plenty of things
    to do.
I have lots of interests and plans too.

I want to go and peruse the mall.
Even though I can only shop at Big and Tall.
I have a career to enhance,
And I'm still in search of romance.

I have financial goals to reach,
And I want to go swimming at the beach.
I will pursue my dreams and goals,
I won't be limited like a goldfish in a bowl.

No longer will my family and friends exploit me,
I will no longer your backup plan be!
I will not be taken advantage of, of this I boast,
My interests must come first and foremost!

Don't Settle for Less

I dated some bums and I know why.
I was told I was fat, so grab what comes by.
You're big and fat, you can't do any better.
If he mistreats you some, it doesn't matter.

No one believed I could get a significant other.
Not my brother, not my sister, not my aunties, not
 even my mother.
Big girls a lot of times get lonely and depressed.
So I decided to settle for less.

The two or three guys that wanted to be my
 friend,
Were so pitiful and such poor excuses for men.
They only wanted to use and leave me high and
 dry,
And caused me so many tears to cry.

They said all the right things when we were alone
I was their whole world when we were on the
 phone.
But they never wanted to be seen with me.
In public, when they saw me they would flee.

We never went out; we were always at home.
I often pretended we were in Paris or Rome.
I just played their games so I would be entertained
They tried my body to gain, but my virginity I
  maintained.

Those jerks were not even worth a dime
I don't know why I even wasted my time.
Every day I would sit on the front porch and pray.
To God my best friend I would say,

Lord please send me a man who's walking in your
  light.
A man like my dad who would treat me right.
Send me a man who would love me in his sight.
A good man who in me would delight.

Then in the following year, March seventh or
  eighth,
The man of my dreams drove through my gates.
He was not ashamed to take me out.
We were hardly ever home, we were all about.

We went to different restaurants, to the movies
  and to malls,
We had picnics at the park and even played
  basketball.

He brought me a rose or a different flower every day,
And always had loving, kind words to say.

He appreciates me even though I was big and fat,
As a matter of fact he loves it like that.
Big girls don't be discouraged, don't settle for less.
Don't settle for any man who doesn't treat you the best!

To make a long story short, see the diamonds on my hand,
God has blessed me with a wonderful man!
So don't be discouraged, don't be dismayed
Don't settle for less, the right man will come your way.

Pain from Your Own

You can't imagine the cruel things that people say,
From "big fat pig," to "your only hope is to be gay."
I think in my life I've heard all the fat jokes,
From elders, from adults; even little kids spoke.

All my classmates mocked me in school.
I was humiliated if I went to the pool.
But nothing pierces my heart with such anguish,
When the fat insults come from the ones you cherish.

What's more devastating when your own,
Put you down and talk about you on the phone.
Oh the pain that I have suffered at the hands of my brothers,
They are ashamed of me, especially in front of others.

My sisters who are supposed to love and help my cause,
Hurl insult after insult, and don't even pause.
Even my dad who is so gentle and sweet,
Think it's cute to call me monkey meat.

What kind of name is that for your child?
How do you expect me to be happy and smile?
How do you expect me to face life with dignity
    and pride?
How do you expect my confidence not to subside?

Even the lady who gave me birth,
Treats me like I don't have worth.
Do you know what it does to a daughter?
To hear unkind words from your own mother.

To hear, "You big fat heifer," ringing in your ears
Devastated my heart and filled my eye with tears.
So many times I've cried, to numerous to
    mention.
Being fat brings out my family's cruel intensions.

Oh the tears that I have cried because of my own.
Because I'm big and fat, I have no place in my
    home.
People wonder why my self-esteem is so low.
It has to do with the lack of love people show.

If they could only walk two steps in my shoes,
And here the snickering, the giggling and the
    boos.

They'll get a taste of the pain I feel inside,
That hurts the heart and destroys my pride

They'll experience the anguish that I feel,
And know the pain that cruel words can cause is
    real.
They'll know how it feels, the emotional pain,
Hearing insults from loved ones with the same
    blood running through our veins.

Jealous Friends

My best friend told me from the beginning,
That I was not going to be in her wedding.
I was not going to be her maid of honor,
Not even a bride's maid in any color.

I did not get upset and I did not complain,
But deep in my heart I cried in pain.
I realized my best friend was of me ashamed,
I realized our friendship was just a game.

I guess the joke was all on me, and always will.
I won't let this get me down, I will press on still.
I know the truth and it causes me great pain.
I won't be in her wedding because of the weight
 I've gained.

I continue to be her friend, but I knew where I
 stood.
Some may say I was foolish, but it all good.
But now all that's changed since I've met this
 man,
Who is my best friend and number one fan.

He helped me to be proud of myself for who I am.

He taught me how to love me and see through
    scams.
Loving yourself is not hard to do,
It's as easy as 1 plus 1 is 2.

Just accept your physical appearance,
Change the things you can with perseverance.
Everyone is beautiful and spectacular,
Avoid friends who suck your blood like Dracula.

I got engaged to this wonderful man,
Then my so-called "best friend" her mouth began
    to ran.
She was angry that I did not ask her to be my
    maid of honor,
But I gave her a chance to be a bride's maid in a
    red color.

This made her indignant and she began to say,
She was not going to be my bride's maid on any
    day.
She was not pleased with the man I would marry,
She wanted me to call it off and say "sorry."

She really thought I was crazy
To break up with a man who treats me like a lady.
She tried to confuse my beliefs.

She wants us to have a meeting with her priest.

She really wanted my fiancé gone,
She even cursed him out on the phone.
She set out to prove that my fiancé was a dog.
She expected him to turn from a prince to a frog.

One day when my fiancé was at my place,
She got dressed up in some sexy lace.
All her private parts were exposed and loose.
She was trying my fiancé to seduce.

But she got her feelings severely hurt,
When she began with my man to flirt.
My man did not even look at her once.
He brought me some flowers then he bounced.

She swore up and down that my man was gay,
Because he did not glance at her once that day.
I know he's not gay, that is just a bunch of lies.
Believe me! I've felt his manhood rise.

But what it all boils down to in the end,
Jealousy was eating at my best friend!
She could not believe that a girl so overweight,
Could meet a man who did truly appreciate.

A man that treated me as a beautiful queen.
A man who beyond doubt loves what he has seen.
My knight in shining armor should be hers,
Not the man of a big oversized girl with curves.

I try to live at peace with all men,
And it's my nature to forgive when others offend.
I'm the bigger person with a wonderful
    personality,
I mean that literally and figuratively.

Now all the girls who I though were my friends,
Have brought our friendships to an end.
They say I've completely changed,
My life has been totally rearranged.

Because now I don't have time for their games,
And my fiancé gets all the blame.
But what others may think really does not matter.
They mistreated and used me because I was fatter.

Now I have a true friend and my king.
He calls me every night and sometimes he sings.
Our friendship has a bond that is so strong.
He loves, honors, and respects me and admits
    when he's wrong.

Mentally Fat

Being fat is constantly on my mind,
I'm fat and it's branded deep down in my mind.
The mind-altering pain that cruel words bring,
Ingrained on my brain with an excruciating sting.
Seeing my fat self in the mirror makes me sick,
I abhor my fat body; I just want to scream and kick.

I understand why people are disgusted by me.
I can't even stand my fat self to see.
I just want to be alone in the dark,
I won't dare go near to a park.
I'm just one big fat blob with pain in my knee.
If I can only get rid of this fat, then I'll be free.

I've got to figure out how to loose this weight,
I wasn't born to be fat, I won't accept this fate.
All these diet programs don't work,
They are just a waste of time, with fluff and perks.
The enemy is the food, but I love to eat!
How will I be able this enemy to defeat?

You will not defeat me food, I still have one trick,
After I eat food, my fingers down my throat I'll stick.

What goes down must come up.
I'm losing weight, now I can shop!
I've gone from a size 30 to a size 9,
But in my mind I'm a size 99.

I've gotten a few compliments sometimes
The guys say that I am fine.
But in my mind I don't believe that,
I still think I'm way too fat.
I'm fat! I still don't like my body!
I'm still too fat and obsequy.

I know what size I need to be,
I actually need to be a size 3.
I hate food; it's the enemy that makes me bloat.
I choke, just thinking about the food that in my
    stomach floats.
I'm so addicted to throwing up, that I can't stop.
My body is fading away, any day now I'll just
drop.

I'm supposed to be happy; living life free and
fancy
Now a size 3; my friends are filled with envy.
But I'm still unhappy and filled with depression,
My fat has left a lasting detrimental impression.
In my mind I still hear a disparaging snicker,

Every whisper, every steer, am I getting thicker.

No matter how petite I get, I still think I'm obese
This drives my eating disorder, which is so hard to cease.
It's hard to believe that with my body now reborn,
I miss the fatness, the hated size I had scorned.
I have the body that I wanted, but my life is at stake,
Because I was not bold enough the jokes to take.

Now with a thin body I have come to realize,
That mockery comes to all sizes.
The funny thing is, people still make fun of me,
I'm a laughing stock because I'm so skinny.
People still whisper, snicker and joke around,
It brings my self-esteem crashing to the ground.

Whether you're short or you're tall,
Whether you have hair or you're bald.
Whether you are black or you're white,
Whether you are smart or not too bright.
Whether you're thin or you're fat,
People will find something to criticize; can you imagine that?

Losing weight this route was not the right way to go,
I must get help from the ones who know.
Now I have to put my name on the doctor's list,
To save my life and continue to exist.
Anorexia I thought a new life would pave,
But it just dug me a smaller grave.

An Essential Element

There are so many diets that I have tried.
Low carb ingredients make horrible tasting pies.
I'm tired of eating salads and vegetables that are green,
I don't want to taste another string bean.
Everyone has the weight loss miracle cure,
So many diet pills just make my stomach sore.

I'm tired of counting calories and carbs,
That's health food propaganda and a bunch of garb!
Taste is one of the most gratifying senses we have,
Not being able to taste good food would drive me mad.
There are so many different diet programs
So many plans that promise to help me lose kilograms.

Whether you are a watcher of the weight,
Or you eat health foods that taste like bait.
Whether you are on the Beverly Hills
Or you are consulting with Dr. Phil.
Whether you are on Atkins High Protein,
Or you are cruising with Kashi GoLean.

Whether you love Cabbage Soup,
Or grooving in the Jenny Craig group.
From Juice fasts to South Beach,
Or whatever diet the nutritionists teach.
No matter what the diet plan or weight management,
There is one common and necessary element.

It's an element that requires a high price,
But in due time it becomes mighty nice.
To have a successful diet you must realize,
That your diet must include exercise!
I know it's not our favorite craze,
But exercise is rejuvenating, you'll be amazed.

Exercise is a necessity whether you are fat or thin,
With consistent exercise the weight battle you'll win.
Exercise doesn't mean participating in a triathlon,
Just take a 20-minute stroll with a loved one.
Be consistent with your exercise every day,
Don't let anything get in your way.

If you can, utilize the local gyms,
They have a variety of equipment to help make the body slim.

Walk the treadmills and ride the bikes,
Choose the Stairmaster that you like.
Dumbbells, barbells, pump those weights,
Burn off the calories from the food you ate.

Don't be ashamed to swim in the pool,
Swimming is effective, easy on your limbs, and it keeps you cool.
Don't be paranoid about how you'll look,
Haven't you been reading this book?
Don't focus on or worry about who is watching,
Just make sure your outfit is cute and matching.

I know it's hard at times, but ignore the stares,
Disregard those indignant glares.
I know we are very sensitive about our appearance,
But no gain will come without perseverance.
Working out is not a fashion show,
Your aim is to sweat; let the perspiration flow.

No pain, no gain; exercise till you perspire,
Keep your eyes on the prize to achieve your desire.
In order for exercise to be effective,
It has to become a habit in the life we live.

The toughest part is getting through the first 2 weeks
Your body will ache, but your sleep will be sweet.

The more you exercise, the more your energy level will soar,
After the first initial soreness, your body will be begging for more.
I know it sounds weird, but try it and see,
A good workout will set your body free.
Exercise tunes the body to its true potential,
It slims you down, all around; it's a true weight loss essential.

Exercise does not only affect our outside body parts,
It strengthens joints, muscles, and even the heart.
Exercise helps our bodies in ways so easy to measure,
It can even help to reduce high blood pressure.
Exercise doesn't only affect the body, but it affects the mind,
It encourages discipline, consistency, and the management of time.

Like it or not, exercise goes a long way,

And the benefits that it returns, for them you can't pay.
It does not matter how you get the exercise,
As long as you stick with it and don't compromise.
From working out at the gym,
To taking a few leisurely swims.

Playing with your kids at the park,
Walking around the track before it gets too dark.
Taking a dancing or yoga class,
Doing sit-ups and squats in the grass.
Just get your body moving,
And don't stop until you are grooving.

You'll quickly notice a major difference,
And knock an inch or two off your appearance.
You'll love the physical and mental benefits,
Just be consistent and stick with it.
Take this important word from the wise,
What does the body good is exercise!

Never Been Out

Once again, I've been stood up!
When will this disappointment ever stop?
The movie started at half past 8;
It's half past 10 and I'm still waiting at the gate.

Why am I being treated this way?
What will the excuse be today?
My mind reflected on times gone by
Remembering specific events with no alibi.

The person that I love and hold so dear,
Never in public seems to be there.
My love always wants to stay in the house,
Shows up secretively at night like a mouse.

When we are alone I'm treated like a queen,
But I can't remember a single place we've been.
The more that I think about the times that we've shared
We've never in a public place appeared.

He calls me several times a day on the phone,
But he won't take me to the park to get a snow cone.

A night on the town is too much to mention,
But when we are alone I get all his attention.

Now the picture has becomes crystal clear,
He keeps me far when others are near.
Now I've finally realized,
We've never gone out because of my size.

I'm going to put an end to all that,
I will not be humiliated because I'm fat.
When we are alone my body you adore,
But you don't want to be seen with me in a store.

He only wants to see me alone at night,
Hey, my dear that's not right!
I refuse to be treated in such a degrading way;
I have pride in my size no matter what others say!

He says that he loves me, but we've never been out,
Please tell me what that is all about?
On second thought, don't even bother to explain,
I'm going to make things extremely plain.

If you don't want to be seen with me in a public place,
You are not a person with dignity and grace.

My time is too precious to waste,
Hit the road, Jack, quickly and with much haste!

He Watched Me Die

Help me! Help me! My body is under siege!
Call 911! Get help quickly please!
Get help! Get help! Why are you standing there?
Get help! I'm in pain! Are you deaf? Can't you
 hear?

I tried to move, but my body was so stiff,
I had some strength, but my weight I couldn't lift.
I was lying on my back, looking straight at my
 man,
He stood there, staring at me, not lending a
 helping hand.

My man just stood there, my eyes filled with
 tears.
Weighing over 350 pounds; I've been sick for 10
 years.
My weight was a burden for way too long,
It affected my health and made things go wrong.

It affected the way my heart did tick
It made me a type-1 diabetic,
My kidneys failed and my blood pressure was
 gigantic,

I have dialysis twice a week at the clinic.

I could not believe the man to whom I had
   dedicated my life,
Would just stand there and do nothing during my
   strife.
For 12 long years I was a committed spouse.
I washed his clothes and kept an immaculate
   house.

I tried to turn my body and my head,
But my weight anchored me to the bed.
I tried to lift my hand to reach the phone,
After struggling to pick it up, there was no dial
   tone.

I can't believe it; he did not pay the phone bill,
How can there be no phone in the house, with
   someone is so ill?
Numbness all over my body roams,
And at the mouth I began to foam.

My life was quickly passing by,
I could not move or speak; all I could do was cry.
He just stood there watching me die,
And I could not understand why?

It's amazing how much of your life you can
  relive,
In just one second when your life is about to give.
I remembered meeting my man by the river,
Oh the sweet deceitful charm he did deliver.

I met him at a low point in my life,
I just became an ex-wife.
My first husband played me for a fool,
And I relied on food the pain to cool.

I was big and so afraid to be alone,
He showered me with attention every night on the
  phone.
My daughter saw right through his act,
But I was too blinded by love to see the facts.

Even when he started the abuse,
I played it off with much amuse.
I separated myself from my family,
I did not want to listen to anybody.

He told me I would not find anyone,
Because I was big and a fat one.
I remember the stories that I was told,
How from my business he stole.

I heard about his extramarital affairs,
We argued and fought; he'd pull out my hair.
But I got to the point were I did not care,
I did not want to be alone, that was my biggest
    fear.

Looking in the mirror my head I would bow,
At this size no one would ever want me now.
I believed all the derogatory things he said to me,
And I ignored anything else said that was
    contrary.

My daughter left home at an early age,
All the abuse I went through had her in rage.
Sadly I did not care because I had my man,
And I was determined by his side to stand.

What a fool I was; I should have left him long
    ago.
He stayed out all night, where he was I did not
    know.
I was so stressed and depressed; I ate all the time,
Because of that heartless cheating man of mine.

He never supported me, my weight to loose,
He always showed up with fattening pies for me
    to choose.

And every time I tried to make it to the track,
He was right there discouraging and holding me
   back.

I quickly began to rack up the pounds,
I still ended up by myself, because he was never
   around.
I wish I had taken my family's advice,
I would end up paying the ultimate price.

Now I'm down to my dying hour,
My throat felt dry and my mouth sour.
He still had control; he still had the power.
My heartbeat was getting faint, but louder.

I could not breathe; my chest was painfully tight,
If I could only turn on my side, I'd be alright.
To shift my weight, my strength could not bear.
My man just stood there watching without a care.

Reality finally set in,
It seems like he would win.
Never true love to me he gave,
He's finally got my money and I'll be dead in the
   grave!

He finally turned around and put on his coat,

And my spirit ascended and began to float.
I could see my man driving in his car,
He drove to my store, which wasn't too far.

When he got to my store he made a phone call,
To his mistress who was slim and tall.
Hey babe, I think my wife is at her end,
I won't see you tonight; I have a funeral to attend.

He looked at his watch every now and then.
Then he said to himself, "Let me call one of her friends".
He called my sister and kindly said,
Sis, I'm coming to get you, your sister is dead.

What did the medic say? What caused her life to stop?
Don't know dear, I'm busy working at the shop.
Sis hung up the phone and called 911,
But it was too late, the damage was already done.

My soul is now in a better place,
Now I fully understand God's amazing grace.
God allowed this tragedy to happen to me,
So that others can learn and set themselves free.

Don't let anyone use your size for their control,

Don't be like a prisoner reporting to a parole.
Don't let the fear of being by yourself,
Make you dependent on someone else.

Don't be scared of being alone,
Utilize your talents and get into a creative zone.
Never let someone destroy your dignity,
Never allow yourself to wallow in self pity.

Try to get yourself as fit as you can,
That fitness may save your life and increase its
    span.
If you are ever lonely and feeling depressed,
Put your trust in God and in His loving arms rest.

If you are in an abusive situation, it's time to take
    a stand,
Don't stay and be unhappy, get out while you can.
Anyone who abuses you is crazy and insane,
Get out while you can, before the blood runs cold
    in your veins.

There is a moral to this poem although it's sad,
If you learn something from it, my soul is glad.

Fat Pride

Pride of life! Life is pride.
Out bodies are fat; we are not going to hide?
We are proud to be fat!
What's so wrong with that?

What's wrong with having meat?
It's actually quite sweet.
We're not inferior!
We're actually quite superior.

We won't buy into the fat frustration!
We'll fuel your life with self-inspiration.
We've already been tagged and badly labeled.
People think that all we do is sit down at the table.

We do everything that other people do,
We just wear a different size shirt, pants or shoe.
It's sad that we've never been given a chance,
We're intelligent, we're witty and we can dance.

We're beautiful both in and out!
If you like the big size, give us a shout!
Your mind has been limited by what you've seen,
The truth is that I am a wonderful human being!

Your mind may be limited by what you see,
But don't project your ignorance toward me.
I'm fat and I'm proud, with positive arrogance.
I'm fat and I'm proud! I will retain my self-confidence!

A Three-Letter Word

It's a word that only has three characters.
It's a word that should not even matter.
It's a word that so simple and plain,
It's a word that has caused so much grief and pain.
It's a word feared by every woman and girl
It's a word loathed by billions all over the world.
It's a word that has made so many cry,
It's a word that has triggered plans to die!
It's a word that is greatly feared,
It's a word that makes supermodels scared.
It's a word that is not associated with beauty.
It's a word that is embraced by comedy.
It's a word that classifies you as a health risk.
It's a word that can stop you from getting a kiss.
It's a word that frustrates women as they shop,
It's a word that brings anger when the zipper pops
It's a word that may have links to heredity
It's a word that has been twisted and used negatively.
It's a word that brings the eating blues.
It's a word that reminds you of weight you have to loose.
It's a word that can keep you from going outside.

It's a word that attacks and strips your pride.
It's a word that poisons your desire for life.
It's a word that upsets every future bride and wife.
It's a word that has so many synonyms.
It's a word with a coveted antonym.

It's a word! It's only a three-letter word!
It's a word not meant to cause so much pain once heard.
It's a word that was only meant to be a description.
It's a word that was not meant to cause devastation.
It's a word not meant to be used as an insult.
It's a word! Don't let it trigger negative results.
It's a word! Don't be terrified of this three-letter word.
It's just a word! In spite of all the dreadful things you've   heard.
It's a word that you can change once you put your mind to it.
It's a word that you can change if you exercise to be fit.
It's a word that you can change with a healthier diet.
It's a word that you can make disappear and be quiet.

It's a word you can change if you just don't quit.
It's a word that you can defeat and outwit.
It's a word! Just another one of society's ploys.
It's a word! Don't let this word steal your joy.
It's a word! Don't let this word get you depressed.
It's a word! Live your life to the fullest.
It's a word! And when this word is in your ears heard,
It's a word! Remember, it's only a three-letter word!

Big Is Beautiful

Everyone desires a lot of things that are big.
People want a big job with a big office.
People want a big car, a big house.
People want a big pool, and go to the biggest schools.
People want a big money bills, and the biggest thrills.
People want big muscles, and the biggest sport players.
People want to go on big shopping sprees.
People want the biggest jewelry, especially the big diamond ring.
People want a big wedding in a big church,
That ends with a big reception, with a big cake.
People want big vegetables, and the biggest fruits.
They want big eggs and the biggest pieces of meat.
We even use chemicals to get the biggest dairy and livestock.
Some people get surgery to get bigger body parts,
They get the big lips, the big buttocks and the biggest breasts.
But when it comes to women the script is reverse,

And big women get humiliated and disgraced the worst.
Society says that big women are not desirable or beautiful,
But if you look around, be truthful you know that's a lie!
Let's look at the facts and the truth will be revealed.
Check the statistics in the surgeon general reports.
This will substantiate and give my words support.
More than 97 million big people exist in the USA.
There are over 1.2 billion big people in the world today.
These millions of big people aren't all monks and nuns,
This means that millions of people find big attractive.
Millions of big people are producing sons and daughters.
Beauty is slowly catching up to its true meaning.
Beauty is not just limited to the tall and the slim.
Big is beautiful and it should not be denied.
Big is a special beauty that society has tried to disguise.
Big is beautiful and it cannot be concealed
Big is beautiful and this beauty must be revealed.
Big is beautiful and is seen all over the world.

Let's give our big people the love and respect they deserve.

Jobs

I'll never get that office job.
I'm always being rejected by some guy name
 Bob.
My size does not allow me to fit into the corporate
 plan,
That would not be if my gender was a man.

My qualifications and credentials, they don't care.
I'm not a slim woman, especially with blonde
 hair.
And knowing this fact makes it tough.
Finding a job with my size is mighty rough.

I'm not the image that corporate men want to see.
Even though there are millions of women just like
 me.
Like they say, "Image is everything."
And what you know doesn't mean a thing.

But I won't give up or despair,
I'm still going to pursue my career.
For every door that gets closed in my face,
I'm going to knock on 10 more with dignity and
 grace.

This world does not have to like me, but it owes
    me a living.
I'll work hard till the sweat starts dripping.
There is a good job out there waiting for me,
I won't rest until someone hires me.

Fat Passion

Right on time, I knew you would not be late.
We both knew our love was destined to be fate.
I knew you'd like the flower petals trailing from
    the door,
All the way up the stairs to the master bedroom's
    floor.

I could not help but admire your sexy voluptuous
    attire,
That glistened in the candle light's bright fire.
I had the champagne on ice,
The filet mignon simmering, with peas and rice.

The table set with fine china, crystal glasses and a
    flower centerpiece so neat.
All that was missing was you to make the evening
    perfect and complete.
We sat for a while and had a great conversation,
But our bodies were trying to get our attention.

We both were nervous and had hesitating fears.
I leaned over and whispered words of passion in
    your ear.
I desired your beautiful big body to be near.

Your face was glowing and your eye had a tear.

Draw closer, let me touch your smooth and tender skin.
I drew you closer and closer in.
I began to explore you adorable face,
Now that you are positioned in the right place.

Your cheeks so warm, oh what passion they did ignite.
Running my fingers through your hair most definitely did excite.
With lips so plump and juicy to kiss,
Burst into flames the passion that I never knew to exist.

With a chunky neck and shoulder smooth and strong,
I knew our passion would burn all night long.
Oh what gorgeous jewels to behold,
A big girls chest is as splendid as gold.

Your breasts are tender, juicy and firm
Your sensitive nipples make my mouth yearn.
Come to me baby, is the voice I hear,
I better cover up now, or my children you will bear.

My hand caresses its way down your back,
No softness did your body lack.
Your belly so pulpy and velvety soft,
Only reinforced my arousal and set things off.

Following your waist line my hands did find,
A muscular, spongy tender behind.
I started to massage your curvy legs,
I would have done anything to touch them, even
 beg!

In my heart I had to confess,
Big is sexy, attractive and stimulatingly the best.
Fat is sensual, enticing and tantalizingly fine.
I'm sorry, my love, you are just blowing my
 mind.

I love the way your body reacts to my touch,
I knew the tension we both were feeling us much.
I was smitten by the sight of you.
You surpassed my greatest fantasies, and that's
 true.

Take your time, let's unwind.
The night's young and we are of the same mind.
As we hugged and embraced,

My heartbeat picked up its pace.

I held you in my arm so tight,
We both knew that this was not right.
We tried to resist the temptation we faced,
From the moment we first embraced.

But temptation was hard to fight,
The sexual attractions, the passionate delight.
Desirous sparks were now roaring flames,
And everything was fair game.

My desire for you was burning me with pain,
But our love and respect I must maintain.
Even though my veins are about to burst,
And if I don't have you right now I'll need a nurse.

You are too precious to be a one-night stand.
I'm thinking long term, I'm thinking wedding bands.
We don't have to have sex to prove our love is real,
Let's sit and have dinner and enjoy our meal.

After dinner we gathered by the fire-side,

I'm down on one knee; would you please be my
    bride?
As I unveiled a three-carat diamond ring,
Surrounded by nine diamond studs that adds to
    the bling.

Fat passion was fueled by true love that will not
    fade,
To love and cherish were the promises we made.
We snuggled up to keep each other warm,
We talked and laughed until the early morning
    dawn.

Plans for our future and the life we'll live,
We both were willing everything to give.
Love with commitment and respect is a must,
Love with dedication and romance is a plus.

Love without trust and truth won't last,
Love with communication and not bringing up
    what's past.
Love with compromise and forgiveness too
Love with passionate sex and lust between us two.

Fat passion that will last our whole life through,
I can hardly wait to marry you.
Your fat passion I can't wait to consume,

I get chills just thinking about our honeymoon.

A life full of romantic and passionate times
I am in love with a fat girl who is exclusively mine.
I love you big girl, with all my heart, body and spirit
You are beyond doubt fantastic, attractive and so terrific!

About the Author

Due to difficult economic times in the West Indies, his family migrated to Brooklyn, NY. Having the support and Christian guidance from his parents, he successfully avoided all of the pitfalls that plague so many inner city kids. After graduating high school, he went on to obtain his Bachelors of Science Degree. He obtained a job as a Software Engineer that gave him an opportunity to do technical writing and newsletter articles. This writing exposure increased his passion for non-technical writing. A few years later he met his beautiful plus size wife, who is the love and joy of his life

Printed in Germany
by Amazon Distribution
GmbH, Leipzig